Oxford
First Atlas

Editorial Adviser
Dr Patrick Wiegand

OXFORD
UNIVERSITY PRESS

Great Clarendon Street, Oxford OX2 6DP

Oxford University Press is a department of the University of Oxford.
It furthers the University's objective of excellence in research, scholarship,
and education by publishing worldwide in

Oxford   New York

Auckland   Cape Town   Dar es Salaam   Hong Kong   Karachi
Kuala Lumpur   Madrid   Melbourne   Mexico City   Nairobi
New Delhi   Shanghai   Taipei   Toronto

With offices in

Argentina   Austria   Brazil   Chile   Czech Republic   France   Greece
Guatemala   Hungary   Italy   Japan   Poland   Portugal   Singapore
South Korea   Switzerland   Thailand   Turkey   Ukraine   Vietnam

Oxford is a registered trade mark of Oxford University Press
in the UK and in certain other countries

ISBN 0 19 832156 2 (hardback)

ISBN 0 19 832155 4 (paperback)

1 3 5 7 9 10 8 6 4 2

Printed in Singapore

Acknowledgements

The publishers would like to thank the following for permission to reproduce the following photographs:
Corbis Images pp 10br, 28cr; Hunting Aerofilms Ltd. p 26br; Hutchison Library pp 29tr (E. Parker), 29tl (Nigel Smith); Impact pp 10tl (J. Hitchings), 28b (Charles Coates), 42tl (Caroline Penn); Mark Mason Studios p 5 all; Mountain Camera pp 10cl (John Cleare), 28t (John Cleare), 29b (Colin Monteath), 42br (Chris Bradley); Panos Pictures p 42bl (Trygve Bolstad); Papilio Photographic p 41; Pictor International p 28cl; Robert Harding pp 10bl (David Martyn Hughes), 10tr (Roy Rainford), 40 (B. O'Connor), 44tl (Tony Stone); Science Photo Library pp 4t, 8tl, 16 (all NRSC Ltd.); Sealand Aerial Photography p 22; Still Pictures pp 10cr (David Drain), 44b (Mark Edwards); The Photolibrary Wales pp 24tr, 24br (both Graham Morley), 24c (Jeremy Moore), 26tr (Brian Tucker), 26tl (Brian Woods), 26bl (David Williams).

Cover image: Tom Van Sant / Geosphere Projection, Santa Monica, Science Photo Library.

The globes on page 5 were supplied by Cambridge Publishing Services.

The illustrations are by Chapman Bounford, Hardlines, and Jon Riley.

The page design is by Adrian Smith.

2 Contents

Maps of the British Isles

Maps of the United Kingdom

Contents 3

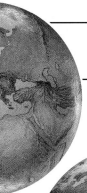
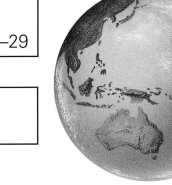
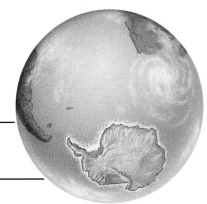
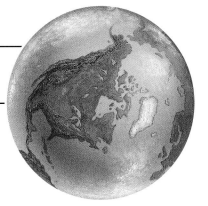

4 Planet Earth

The Earth is a **planet** in space.

It is round like a ball.

If you look at the Earth from space you can see land, sea, and clouds.

You cannot see countries.

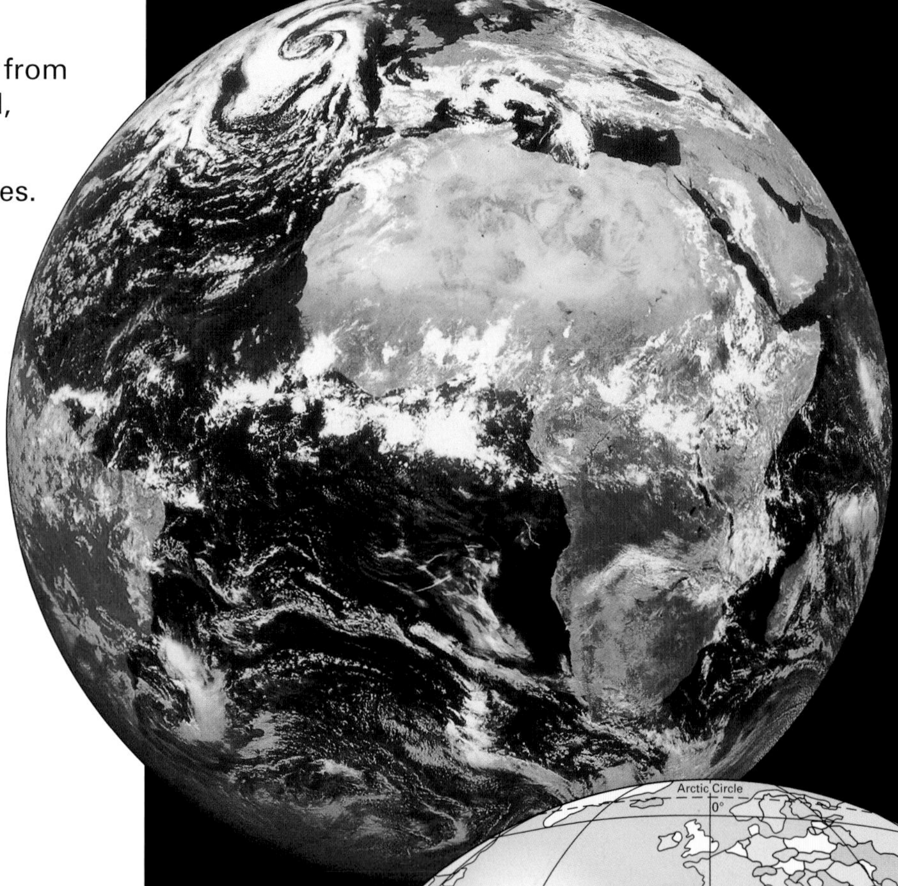

To see countries you need a map.

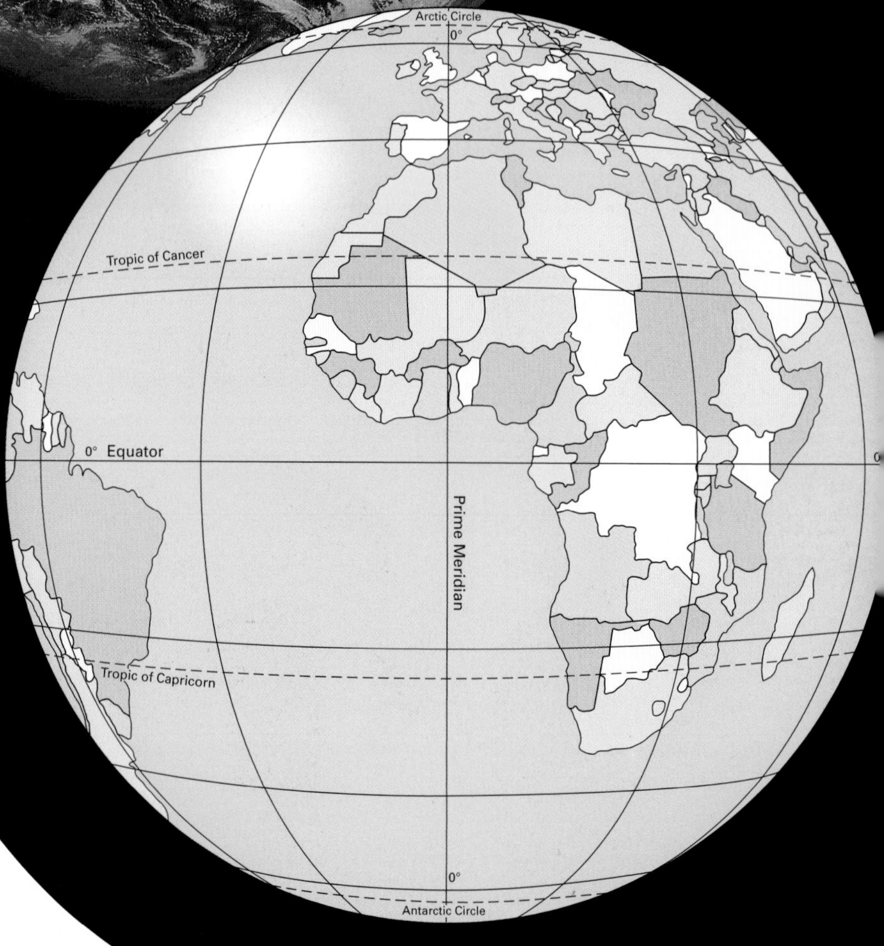

There are imaginary lines round the Earth. These help us describe where places are.

Some of the lines have special names.

The line around the middle of the Earth is called the **Equator**.

Arctic Circle
0°
Tropic of Cancer
0° Equator
Prime Meridian
Tropic of Capricorn
0°
Antarctic Circle

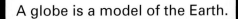

A globe is a model of the Earth.

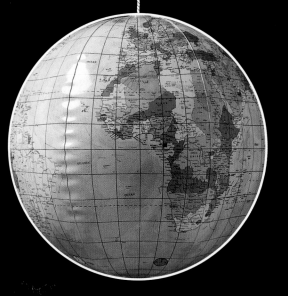

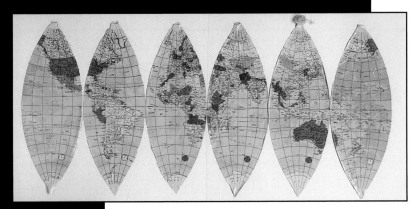

These strips have been cut from a globe and laid flat.

They make a world map.

The map is not easy to use because there are gaps in it.

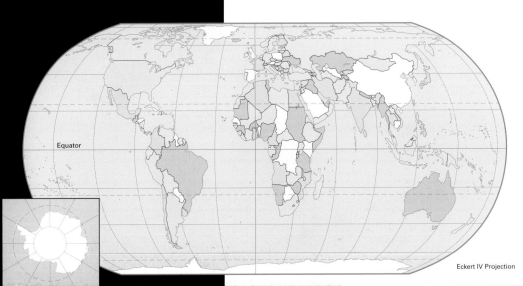

Equator

Eckert IV Projection

Here is a better world map. Some of the land shapes have had to be stretched.

A world map like this does not show Antarctica very well.

So Antarctica is shown here on a separate map.

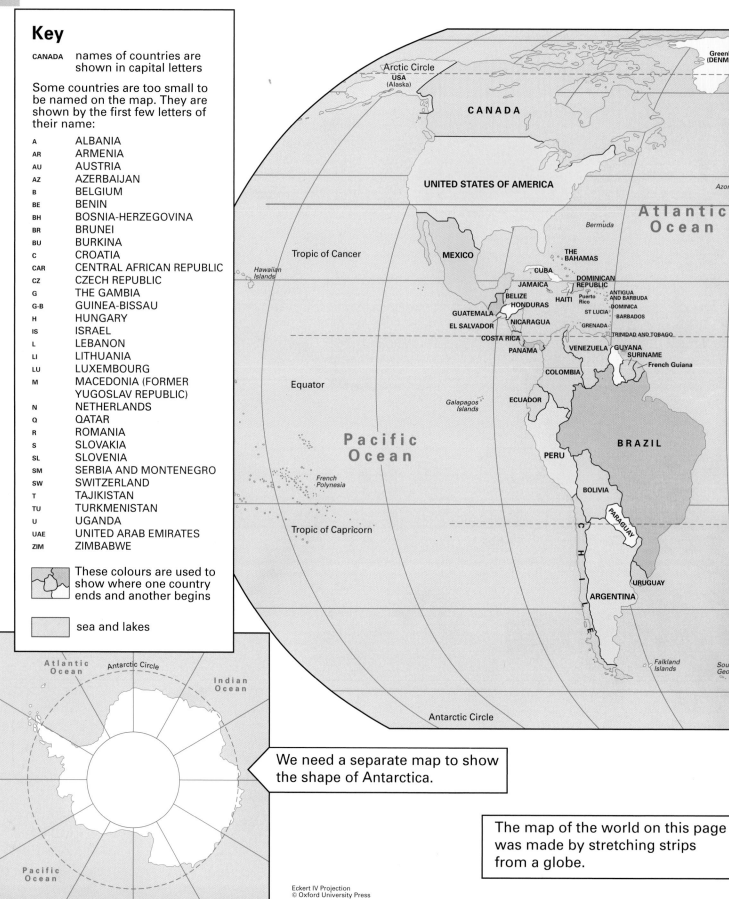

Key

CANADA   names of countries are shown in capital letters

Some countries are too small to be named on the map. They are shown by the first few letters of their name:

A	ALBANIA
AR	ARMENIA
AU	AUSTRIA
AZ	AZERBAIJAN
B	BELGIUM
BE	BENIN
BH	BOSNIA-HERZEGOVINA
BR	BRUNEI
BU	BURKINA
C	CROATIA
CAR	CENTRAL AFRICAN REPUBLIC
CZ	CZECH REPUBLIC
G	THE GAMBIA
G-B	GUINEA-BISSAU
H	HUNGARY
IS	ISRAEL
L	LEBANON
LI	LITHUANIA
LU	LUXEMBOURG
M	MACEDONIA (FORMER YUGOSLAV REPUBLIC)
N	NETHERLANDS
Q	QATAR
R	ROMANIA
S	SLOVAKIA
SL	SLOVENIA
SM	SERBIA AND MONTENEGRO
SW	SWITZERLAND
T	TAJIKISTAN
TU	TURKMENISTAN
U	UGANDA
UAE	UNITED ARAB EMIRATES
ZIM	ZIMBABWE

These colours are used to show where one country ends and another begins

sea and lakes

We need a separate map to show the shape of Antarctica.

The map of the world on this page was made by stretching strips from a globe.

Eckert IV Projection
© Oxford University Press

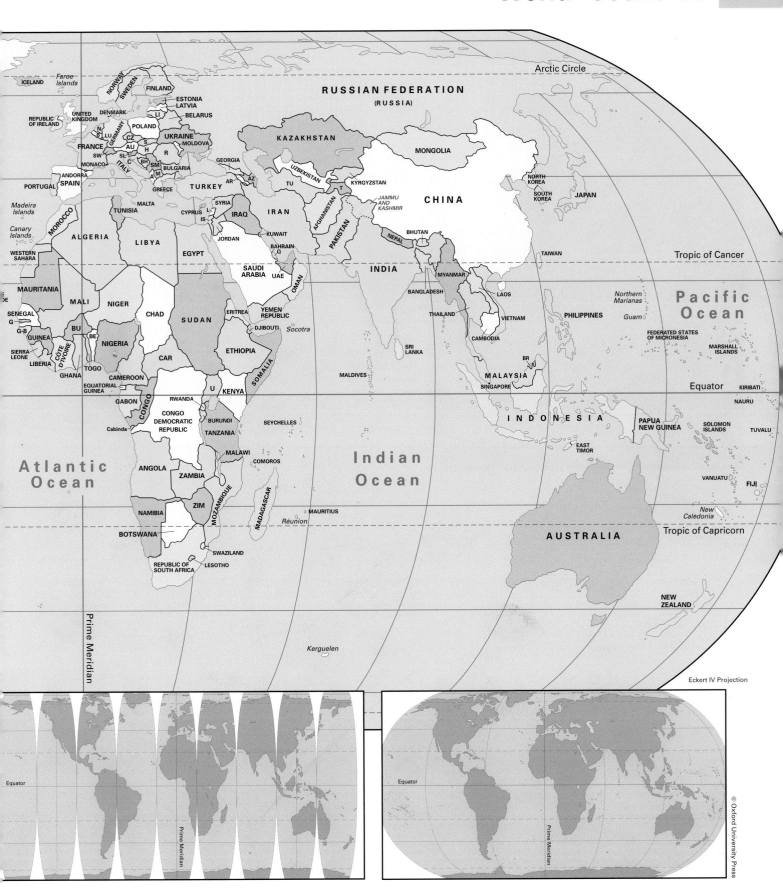

Arctic Circle

ICELAND
Faroe Islands
NORWAY
SWEDEN
FINLAND
ESTONIA
LATVIA
DENMARK
BELARUS
LI
REPUBLIC OF IRELAND
UNITED KINGDOM
POLAND
N
B
LU
GERMANY
CZ
UKRAINE
MOLDOVA
FRANCE
SW
AU
H
R
S
MONACO
ITALY
C
BH
SM
A
M
BULGARIA
ANDORRA
SPAIN
GREECE
PORTUGAL
Madeira Islands
Canary Islands
MOROCCO
TUNISIA
MALTA
CYPRUS
IS
SYRIA
LEBANON
IRAQ
JORDAN
BAHRAIN
Q
UAE
OMAN

RUSSIAN FEDERATION (RUSSIA)

KAZAKHSTAN
GEORGIA
AR
AZ
TU
UZBEKISTAN
KYRGYZSTAN
T
TURKEY
IRAN
AFGHANISTAN
PAKISTAN
JAMMU AND KASHMIR
MONGOLIA
CHINA
NORTH KOREA
SOUTH KOREA
JAPAN

ALGERIA
LIBYA
EGYPT
WESTERN SAHARA
MAURITANIA
MALI
NIGER
CHAD
SUDAN
SENEGAL
G
G-B
GUINEA
BU
BE
NIGERIA
SIERRA LEONE
LIBERIA
CÔTE D'IVOIRE
GHANA
TOGO
CAR
CAMEROON
EQUATORIAL GUINEA
ERITREA
DJIBOUTI
Socotra
ETHIOPIA
SOMALIA
U
KENYA
YEMEN REPUBLIC
SAUDI ARABIA
KUWAIT
DE

Tropic of Cancer

NEPAL
BHUTAN
INDIA
BANGLADESH
MYANMAR
LAOS
THAILAND
VIETNAM
CAMBODIA
SRI LANKA
MALDIVES

TAIWAN
Northern Marianas
Guam
PHILIPPINES
FEDERATED STATES OF MICRONESIA
MARSHALL ISLANDS

Pacific Ocean

MALAYSIA
SINGAPORE
BR
INDONESIA
EAST TIMOR
PAPUA NEW GUINEA
SOLOMON ISLANDS

Equator
KIRIBATI
NAURU
TUVALU

GABON
CONGO
Cabinda
CONGO DEMOCRATIC REPUBLIC
RWANDA
BURUNDI
TANZANIA
MALAWI
SEYCHELLES
COMOROS

Indian Ocean

Atlantic Ocean

ANGOLA
ZAMBIA
ZIM
MOZAMBIQUE
NAMIBIA
BOTSWANA
MADAGASCAR
Réunion
MAURITIUS
SWAZILAND
REPUBLIC OF SOUTH AFRICA
LESOTHO

VANUATU
FIJI
New Caledonia

AUSTRALIA
Tropic of Capricorn

NEW ZEALAND

Prime Meridian

Kerguelen

Eckert IV Projection

Equator

Prime Meridian

Equator

Prime Meridian

These are the British Isles seen from space.

Great Britain and Ireland are **islands**.

They are land with sea all around.

These two large islands, together with many small ones, make the **British Isles**.

Ireland

Great Britain

It is about 1000 kilometres from John o'Groats to Land's End, as the crow flies.

This journey would take:

about **2 hours** by air

about **2 days** by car

about **40 days** to walk

John o'Groats

Land's End

The British Isles are small compared to many other places in the world.

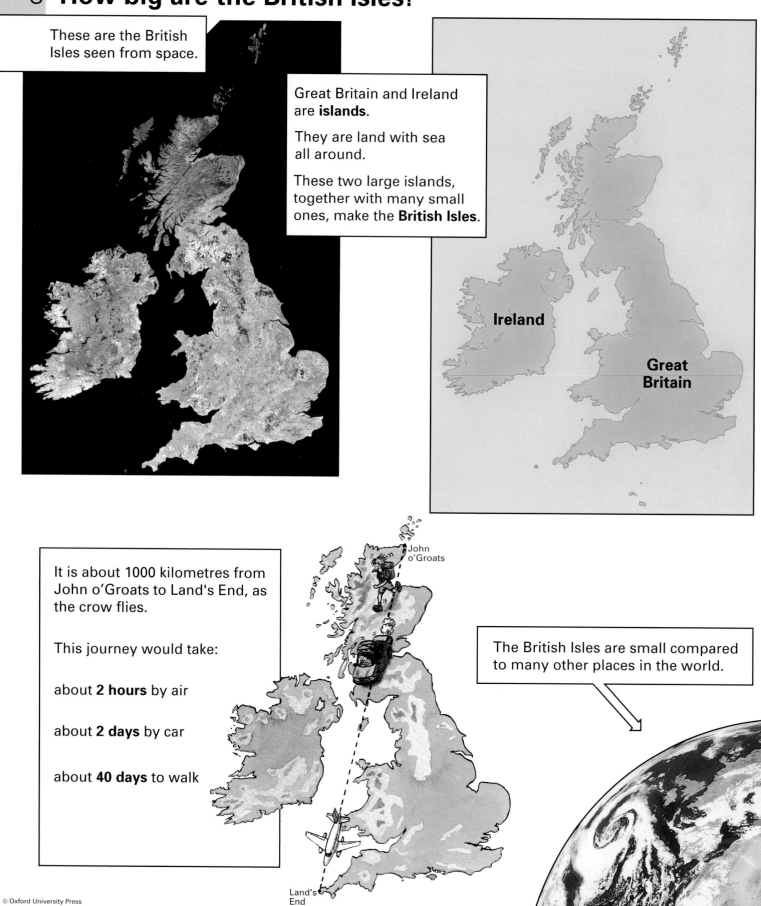

Key

- ■ Capital cities
- England
- Wales
- Scotland
- Northern Ireland
- Republic of Ireland
- Channel Islands
- Isle of Man

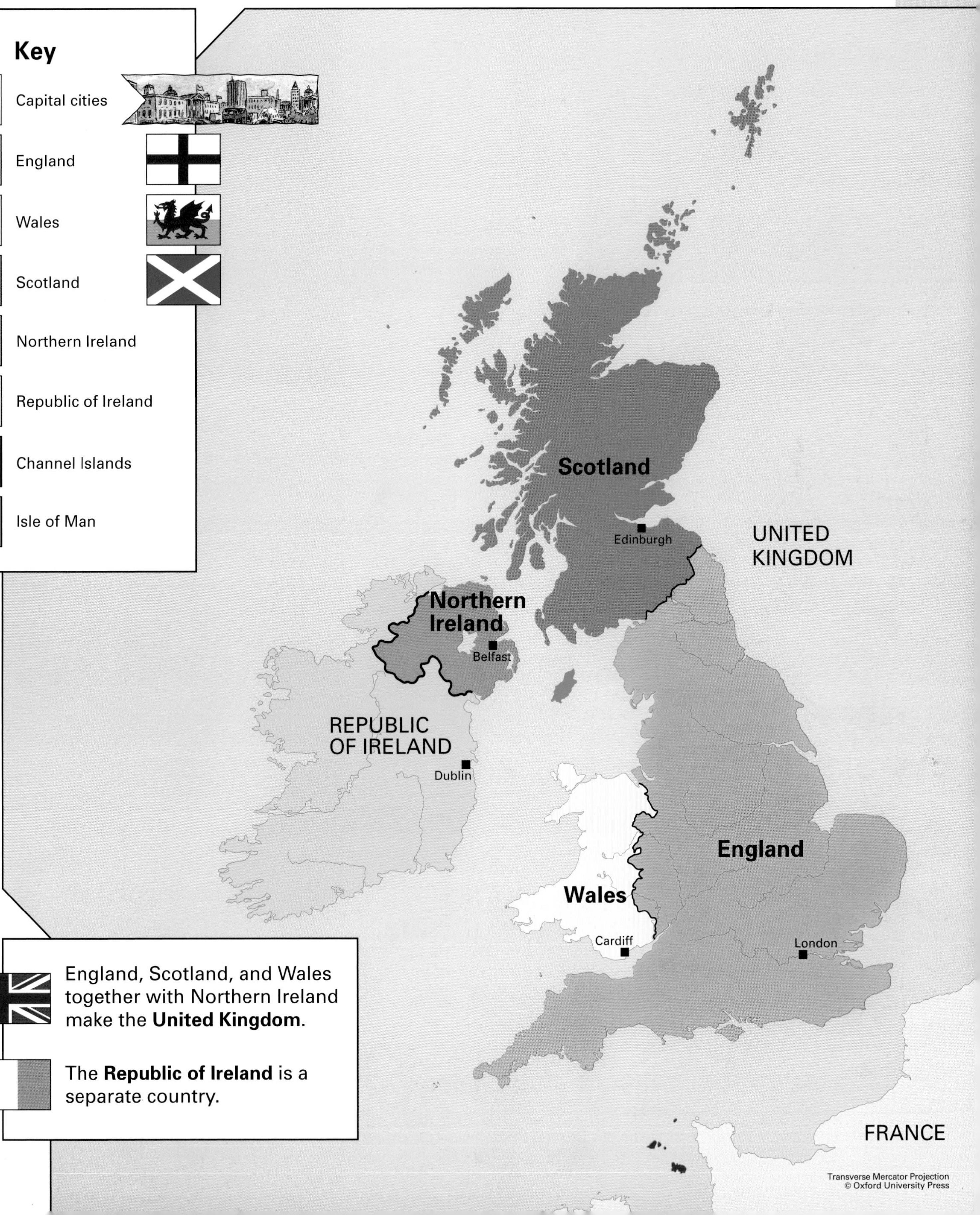

Scotland

Edinburgh ■

UNITED KINGDOM

Northern Ireland

Belfast ■

REPUBLIC OF IRELAND

Dublin ■

England

Wales

Cardiff ■

London ■

FRANCE

England, Scotland, and Wales together with Northern Ireland make the **United Kingdom**.

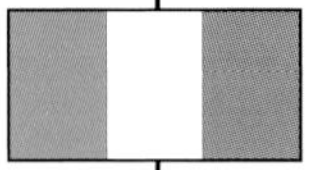

The **Republic of Ireland** is a separate country.

Transverse Mercator Projection
© Oxford University Press

highest peaks

from these you can see a long way in all directions

Snowdonia, Wales

mountains

steep, rocky slopes

Grampian Mountains, Scotland

moors and uplands

high, wind-swept places with heather and rough grass

Exmoor, England

hills

smooth slopes and gentle valleys

Pennines, England

low lands

mostly flat, marshy land with wide rivers

Cotswolds, England

rivers

rainwater runs downhill to collect in rivers which flow to the sea

River Wye, Wales

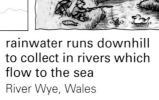

Key

- highest peaks
- mountains
- moors and uplands
- hills
- low lands
- rivers
- sea

ATLANTIC

OCEAN

NORTHWEST HIGHLANDS

Great Glen

River Spey

River Dee

GRAMPIAN MOUNTAINS

Ben Nevis ▲

River Clyde

SOUTHERN UPLANDS

River Tweed

River Tyne

N o r t h

S e a

River Bann

ANTRIM MOUNTAINS

Loch Neagh

River Erne

Slieve Donard ▲

LAKE DISTRICT

Scafell Pike ▲

PENNINES

NORTH YORK MOORS

River Aire

Irish Sea

Loch Corrib

River Shannon

River Liffey

WICKLOW MOUNTAINS

River Barrow

River

Snowdon ▲

River Trent

CAMBRIAN MOUNTAINS

River Severn

River Great Ouse

River Blackwater

Carrantuohill ▲

BRECON BEACONS

River Wye

River Avon

COTSWOLD HILLS

CHILTERN HILLS

River Thames

NORTH DOWNS

EXMOOR

SOUTH DOWNS

DARTMOOR

E n g l i s h   C h a n n e l

Transverse Mercator Projection
© Oxford University Press

Our weather in summer

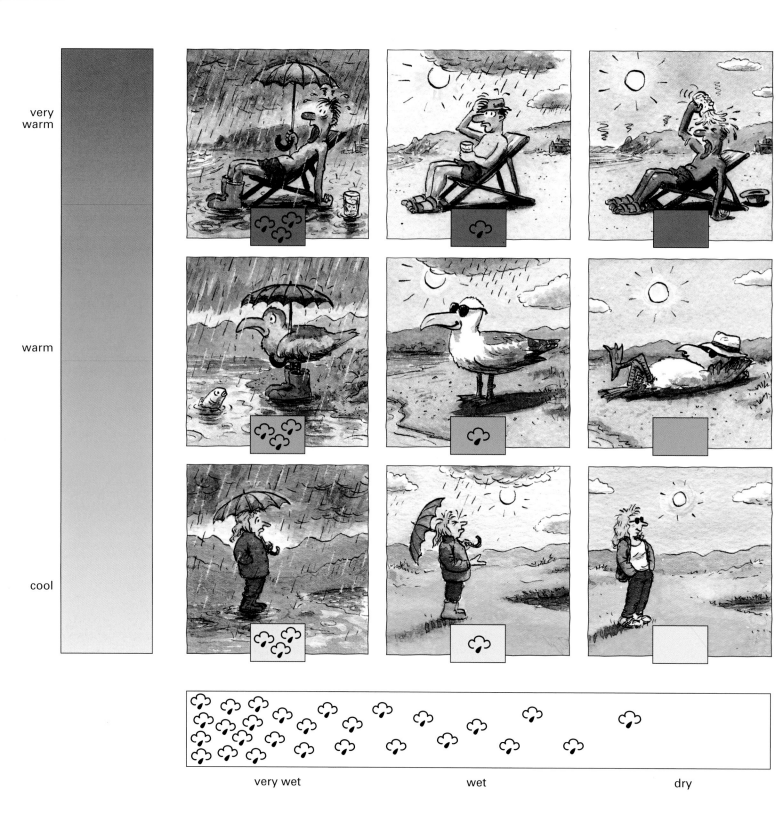

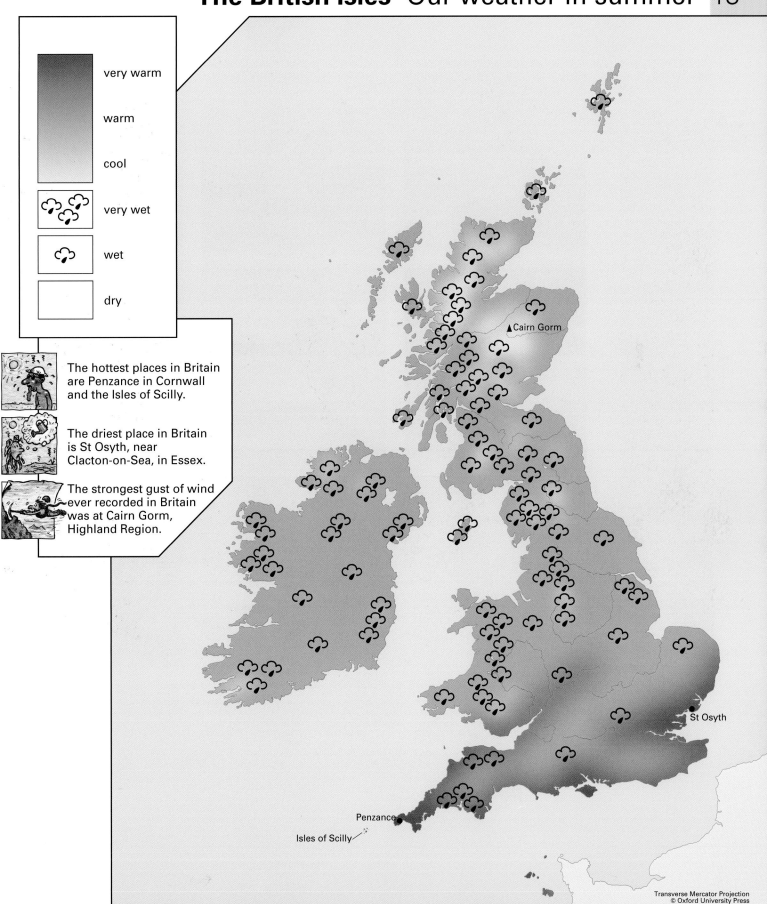

very warm

warm

cool

very wet

wet

dry

The hottest places in Britain are Penzance in Cornwall and the Isles of Scilly.

The driest place in Britain is St Osyth, near Clacton-on-Sea, in Essex.

The strongest gust of wind ever recorded in Britain was at Cairn Gorm, Highland Region.

▲Cairn Gorm

St Osyth

Penzance

Isles of Scilly

Transverse Mercator Projection
© Oxford University Press

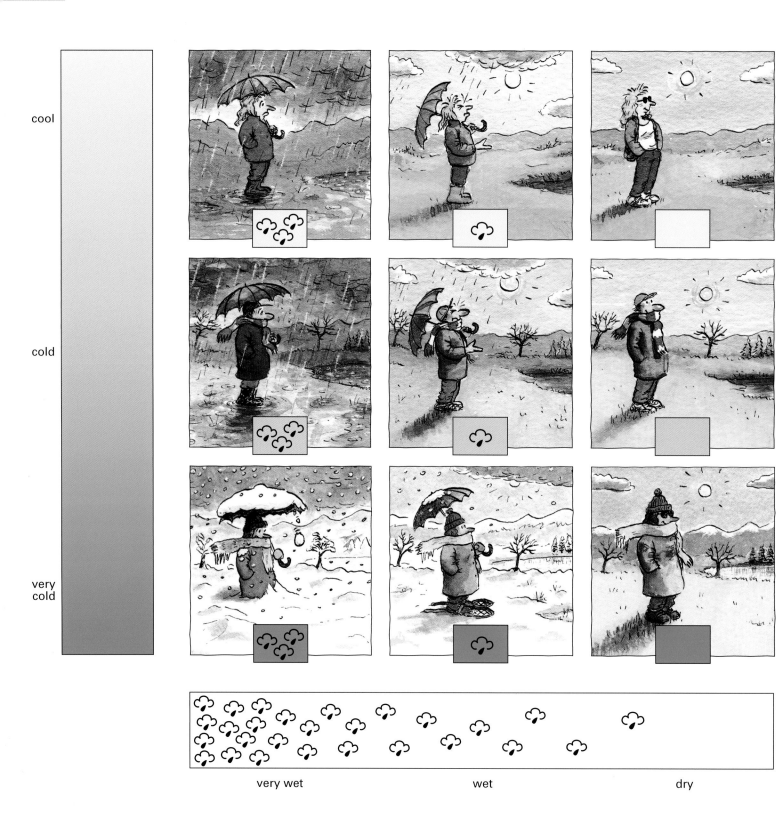

cool

cold

very
cold

very wet   wet   dry

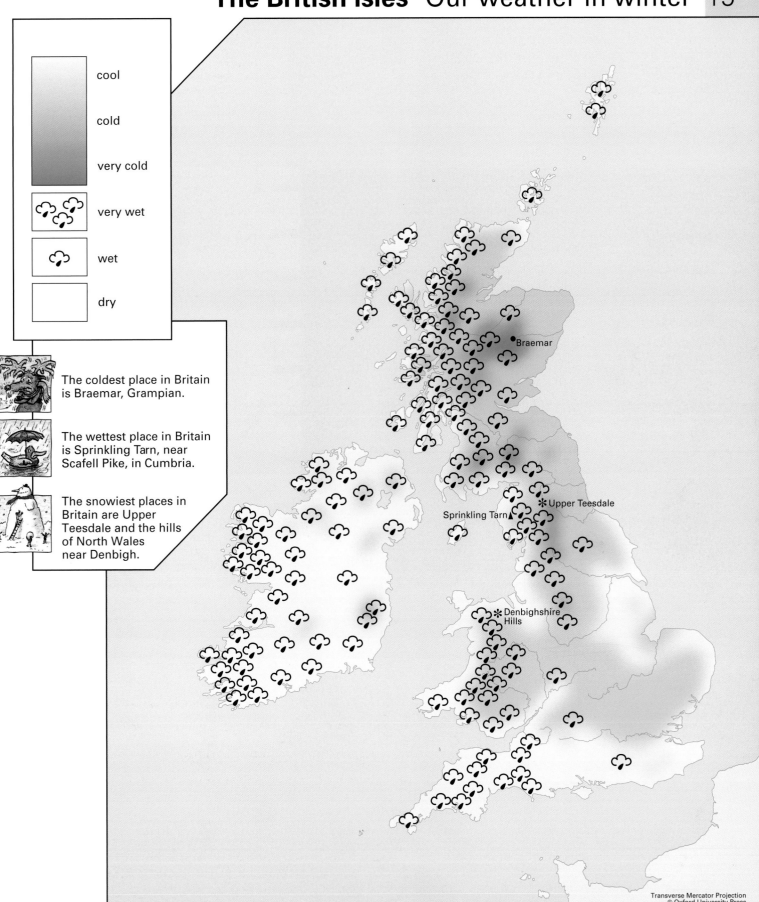

cool

cold

very cold

very wet

wet

dry

The coldest place in Britain is Braemar, Grampian.

The wettest place in Britain is Sprinkling Tarn, near Scafell Pike, in Cumbria.

The snowiest places in Britain are Upper Teesdale and the hills of North Wales near Denbigh.

Braemar

* Upper Teesdale

Sprinkling Tarn▲

* Denbighshire Hills

Pictures from space show lots of detail but it is hard to see each town and road.

Maps pick out the most important places and show their names.

Key

lines marking the edge of a country	
motorways and major roads	
railway	
main airport	
town	
large town	
largest built-up area	
river	
lake	
peak or highest point	
mountains	
moors and uplands	
hills	
low lands	
land below sea level	

Transverse Mercator Projection
© Oxford University Press

	B	C	D	E	F	G	H	J

5

A

4

3

2

1

N

A T L A N T I C

O C E A N

Rona

Shetland Islands

Herma Ness

Unst

Fetlar

Yell

Out Skerries

Whalsay

Mainland

Bressay

Foula

Scalloway • Lerwick

Sumburgh Head

Fair Isle

Papa Westray
North Ronaldsay
Westray
Rousay
Sanday
Orkney Islands
Eday
Stronsay
Mainland
Shapinsay
Stromness •
Kirkwall
Hoy
South Ronaldsay
Pentland Firth
Duncansby Head
John o' Groats
• Thurso
• Wick

N o r t h

S e a

Cape Wrath

Butt of Lewis

The Minch

Outer Hebrides

Stornoway
Lewis

Clisham
799m

Harris
Scalpay

Little Minch

Pabbay
Berneray

North Uist

Benbecula

South Uist

Barra

Mingulay

...lda

Ben More Assynt 998m

Loch Shin

NORTHWEST HIGHLANDS

Dornoch Firth

Tarbat Ness

Ullapool •

Sgurr Mor 1109m
Ben Wyvis 1046m

Moray Firth

Dingwall •

Fraserburgh

Peterhead

Portree •
Raasay

Skye
CUILLIN HILLS
1009m

Kyle of Lochalsh •

Carn Eige 1183m

Inverness

Elgin

Loch Ness

Aviemore

River Spey

River Deveron

River Don

CAIRNGORMS

Fort Augustus
MONADHLIATH MOUNTAINS

Ben Macdui 1310m

Canna

Rhum

Sound of Sleat

Mallaig •

Eigg

Great Glen

Braemar •

River Dee

⊕ **Aberdeen**

Fort William
Ben Nevis 1344m

G R A M P I A N   M O U N T A I N S

River North Esk

Montrose

River South Esk
Forfar

Coll

Tiree

Loch Linnhe

Ben Cruachan 1126m

Loch Rannoch

Loch Tay

River Tay

SIDLAW HILLS

Arbroath

Dundee

Ulva

Mull

S C O T L A N D

Iona

Oban •

Loch Awe

Inner Hebrides

Firth of Lorn

Colonsay

Jura

Loch Fyne

Loch Lomond

R. Forth

Perth •

Stirling

St Andrews •

Glenrothes •

Kirkcaldy •

© Oxford University Press

Key

∼	lines marking the edge of a country
∼	motorways and major roads
∼	railway
⊕	main airport
·	town
●	large town
▨	largest built-up area
∼	river
◗	lake
▲	peak or highest point
	mountains
	moors and uplands
	hills
	low lands
	land below sea level

Transverse Mercator Projection
© Oxford University Press

Key

~~	lines marking the edge of a country
~~	motorways and major roads
~~	railway
⊕	main airport
·	town
●	large town
	largest built-up area
	river
	lake
▲	peak or highest point
	mountains
	moors and uplands
	hills
	low lands
	land below sea level

Grid references: J K L M N, 6 5 4 3 2

Map labels (England):
Scunthorpe, Grimsby, Spurn Head, River Humber, Louth, Mablethorpe, Lincoln, LINCOLN WOLDS, Newark-on-Trent, Skegness, Wells-next-the-Sea, Boston, Nottingham, Grantham, The Wash, King's Lynn, Cromer, River Bure, Spalding, Wisbech, THE FENS, River Wensum, Great Yarmouth, Norwich, Corby, Peterborough, Thetford, River Waveney, Lowestoft, Kettering, R. Great Ouse, Ely, Southwold, Northampton, Bury St Edmunds, Cambridge, Bedford, ENGLAND, Aldeburgh, Milton Keynes, River Stour, Ipswich, Felixstowe, Luton, Harwich, Welwyn Garden City, Harlow, Colchester, St Osyth, Aylesbury, St Albans, Chelmsford, CHILTERN HILLS, Watford, Basildon, Southend-on-Sea, Slough, London, Gravesend, Margate, Windsor, Sheerness, Reading, Gillingham, Canterbury, Woking, Reigate, Maidstone, NORTH DOWNS, Deal, Guildford, Redhill, Ashford, Dover, Crawley, THE WEALD, Royal Tunbridge Wells, Folkestone, Horsham, R. Arun, R. Medway, R. Lea, SOUTH DOWNS, Havant, Brighton, Hastings, Bognor Regis, Worthing, Eastbourne, Newhaven, Beachy Head, Strait of Dover

North Sea

France / Belgium labels:
Oostende, Nieuwpoort, Dunkerque, Calais, BELGIUM, Poperinge, Cassel, St-Omer, Armentières, Lillers, Boulogne-sur-Mer, Montreuil-sur-Mer, Bruay-en-Artois, Lens, le Touquet-Paris-Plage, Hesdin, Arras, Berck-Plage, FRANCE, Doullens, le Tréport, Abbeville, River Somme, Dieppe, St Valery-en-Caux, Blangy-sur-Bresle, Amiens, St Quentin, Fécamp, Etretat, Neufchâtel-en-Bray, Poix-de-Picardie, Roye, Montdidier, Baie de la Seine, Bolbec, Yvetot, Forges-les-Eaux, Gournay-en-Bray, Laon, Noyon, le Havre, Honfleur, Pont-Audemer, Beauvais, Compiègne, Clermont, Oise, Soissons, Deauville-les-Bains, Rouen, River Seine, Gisors, Bayeux, Caen, Cabourg, Lisieux, Louviers, Vernon, Senlis, Château-Thierry, Paris

Transverse Mercator Projection
© Oxford University Press

REPUBLIC OF IRELAND

Where people live

Large towns and built-up areas have lots of houses, schools, shops, offices, and factories.

This photograph shows part of Cardiff.

Most people in Britain live and work in large towns and built-up areas.

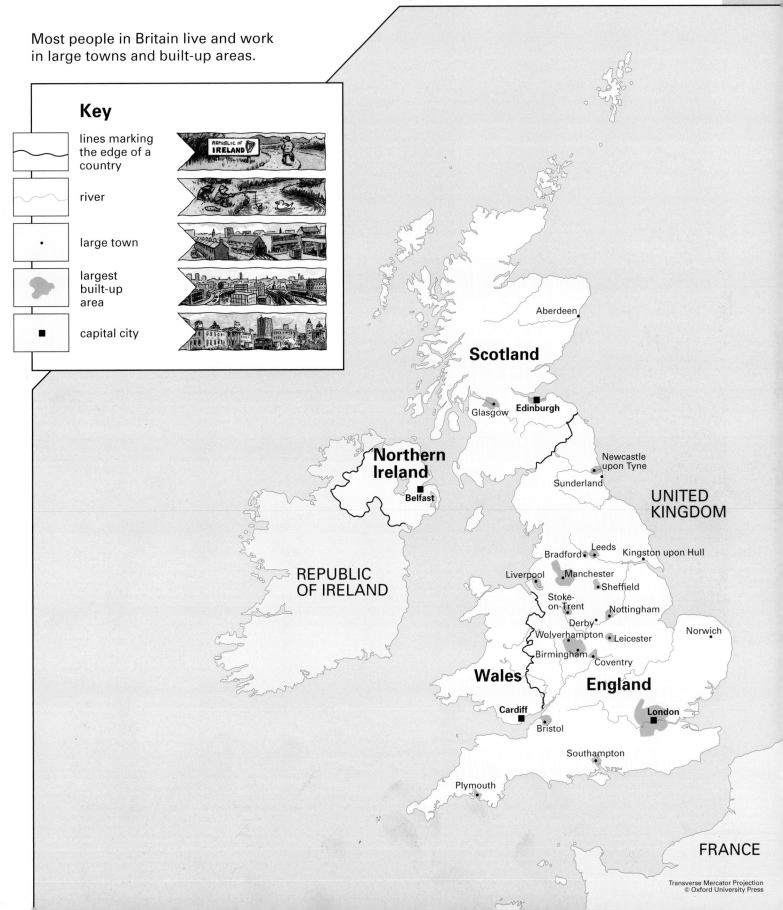

Key

～～	lines marking the edge of a country
～～	river
•	large town
⬤	largest built-up area
■	capital city

REPUBLIC OF IRELAND

Scotland

Aberdeen

Glasgow Edinburgh

Northern
Ireland

Belfast

Newcastle
upon Tyne

Sunderland

UNITED
KINGDOM

REPUBLIC
OF IRELAND

Leeds

Bradford

Kingston upon Hull

Liverpool Manchester

Sheffield

Stoke-
on-Trent

Nottingham

Derby

Wolverhampton Leicester

Norwich

Birmingham

Coventry

Wales

England

Cardiff

London

Bristol

Southampton

Plymouth

FRANCE

Transverse Mercator Projection
© Oxford University Press

farmland

farmers use the land to produce food by growing crops and keeping animals

 forest

forest land is used to grow trees for timber

 coast

much land at the edge of the sea is used for holidays

Key

lines marking the edge of a country

built-up areas

farmland

forest and woodland

mountain holidays

sandy beaches

REPUBLIC OF IRELAND

North Sea

Northwest Highlands

Grampian Mountains

Southern Uplands

Kielder Forest

Pennines

Manchester

North Wales

East Anglia

Birmingham

London

West Country

South Coast

ATLANTIC OCEAN

Transverse Mercator Projection
© Oxford University Press

railway

motorway

airport

car ferry

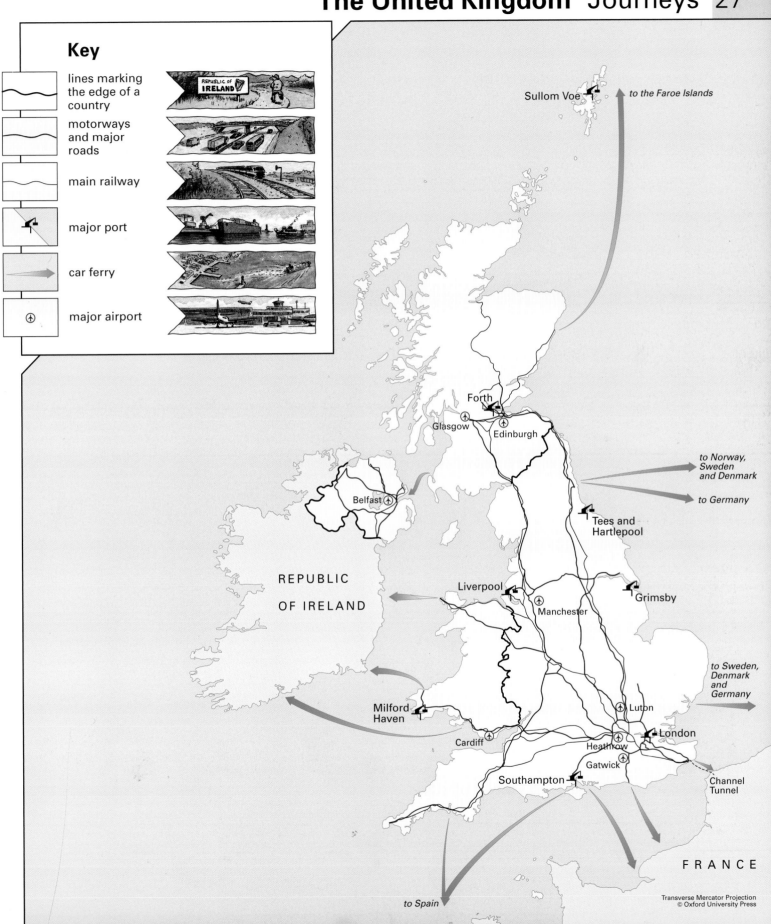

Key

~	lines marking the edge of a country
~	motorways and major roads
~	main railway
⚑	major port
➤	car ferry
⊕	major airport

REPUBLIC OF IRELAND

Sullom Voe

to the Faroe Islands

Forth

Glasgow   Edinburgh

Belfast

to Norway, Sweden and Denmark

to Germany

Tees and Hartlepool

REPUBLIC

OF IRELAND

Liverpool

Manchester

Grimsby

to Sweden, Denmark and Germany

Milford Haven

Luton

Cardiff

London

Heathrow

Gatwick

Channel Tunnel

Southampton

FRANCE

to Spain

Transverse Mercator Projection
© Oxford University Press

mountains
Himalayas, Nepal

desert Kalahari, southern Africa

savannah Masai Mara, Kenya

marsh
Okavango Swamp,
Botswana

cold forest
Coniferous forest, Switzerland

hot forest Amazon Rainforest, Brazil

The photographs show different environments.
They are our natural surroundings.

The matching symbols are used on the maps on pages 30-39.

ice and icebergs Antarctica

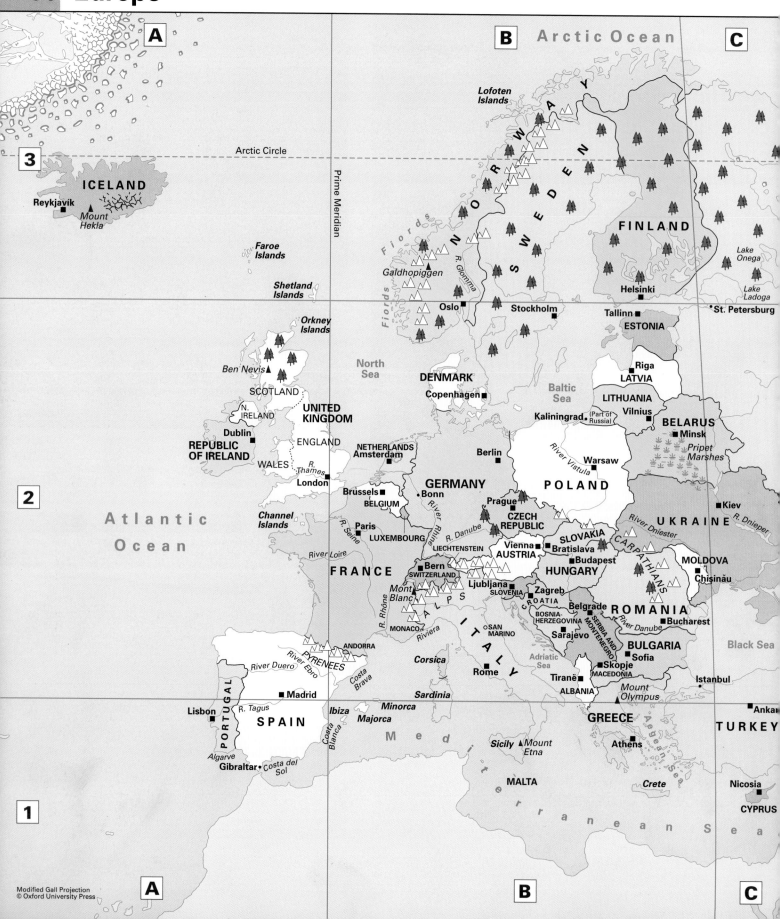

A   **B**   **C**

3

Arctic Circle

ICELAND

Reykjavik ■

▲ Mount
Hekla

Faroe
Islands

Shetland
Islands

Lofoten
Islands

N O R W A Y

S W E D E N

FINLAND

Lake
Onega

Lake
Ladoga

Fiords

Galdhøpiggen ▲

R. Glomma

Oslo ■

Stockholm ■

Helsinki ■

Tallinn ■

● St. Petersburg

ESTONIA

2

**Atlantic
Ocean**

Orkney
Islands

Ben Nevis ▲

SCOTLAND

N.
IRELAND

UNITED
KINGDOM

Dublin ■

REPUBLIC
OF IRELAND

ENGLAND

WALES

R.
Thames

London ■

North
Sea

DENMARK

Copenhagen ■

Baltic
Sea

Riga ■
LATVIA

LITHUANIA

Vilnius ■

Kaliningrad ■
(Part of
Russia)

BELARUS

Minsk ■

Pripet
Marshes

Brussels ■

BELGIUM

NETHERLANDS

Amsterdam ■

GERMANY

Berlin ■

Bonn ●

River Rhine

POLAND

River Vistula

Warsaw ■

Kiev ■

UKRAINE

R. Dnieper

Channel
Islands

Paris ■

R. Seine

LUXEMBOURG

Prague ■

CZECH
REPUBLIC

SLOVAKIA

Bratislava ■

River Danube

R. Danube

Vienna ■

AUSTRIA

LIECHTENSTEIN

HUNGARY

Budapest ■

CARPATHIANS

River Dniester

MOLDOVA

Chisinău ■

River Loire

FRANCE

Bern ■

SWITZERLAND

Mont
Blanc ▲

A L P S

Ljubljana ■

SLOVENIA

Zagreb ■

CROATIA

Belgrade ■

SERBIA AND
MONTENEGRO

ROMANIA

Bucharest ■

River Danube

R. Rhône

MONACO

Riviera

I T A L Y

SAN
MARINO ●

Sarajevo ■

BOSNIA-
HERZEGOVINA

Adriatic
Sea

BULGARIA

Sofia ■

Black
Sea

PYRENEES

ANDORRA

River Ebro

Costa
Brava

Corsica

Rome ■

Skopje ■
MACEDONIA

Tiranë ■

ALBANIA

Mount
Olympus ▲

Istanbul ●

River Duero

Madrid ■

PORTUGAL

SPAIN

Lisbon ■

R. Tagus

Ibiza

Minorca

Majorca

Sardinia

Sicily

▲ Mount
Etna

GREECE

Athens ■

Aegean Sea

TURKEY

Anka ■

Algarve

Gibraltar ●

Costa del
Sol

Costa
Blanca

M e d i t e r r a n e a n   S e a

MALTA

Crete

Nicosia ■

CYPRUS

1

A   **B**   **C**

C
D
Arctic Ocean
Barents Sea

Countries in the European Union

3

North Dvina River

U R A L   M O U N T A I N S

RUSSIAN FEDERATION
(RUSSIA)

River Volga

■ Moscow

2

Caspian Sea

Mount Elbrus ▲
CAUCASUS
GEORGIA
■ Tbilisi

TAURUS MOUNTAINS

1

Key

ITALY	names of countries are in capital letters		marsh
■	capital cities		ice on land / ice on sea
•	other big cities		icebergs
~~	the biggest rivers		
▲	the highest peaks		
△	mountains		
🌲	cold forest		

C
D

A   **B**   **C**   **D**   **E**

5

Barents Sea

Arctic Circle

RUSSIAN FEDERATION (RUSSIA)

Yenisey River

River Ob

URAL MOUNTAINS

River Volga

Angara River

River Lena

■ Moscow

Lake Baykal

Sea of Okhot

4

Astana ■

River Irtysh

KAZAKHSTAN

Lake Balkhash

ALTAI MOUNTAINS

Ulan Bator ■

MONGOLIA

River Amur

Aral Sea

GOBI DESERT

Black Sea

CAUCASUS

Caspian Sea

Almaty •

Bishkek

Hokkaido

ARMENIA

Baku

UZBEKISTAN

Tashkent ■

KYRGYZSTAN

Beijing ■

NORTH KOREA

Sea of Japan

Yerevan •

Hwang Ho River

Mount Ararat

AZERBAIJAN

Dushanbe ■

Communism Peak

Tianjin •

Pyongyang ■

JAPA

TURKMENISTAN

TAJIKISTAN

Seoul ■

SOUTH KOREA

Tokyo ■

R. Euphrates

R. Tigris

Ashgabat ■

Mount Demavend

AFGHANISTAN

Mount K2

CHINA

Mount Fuji ▲

Honshu

Beirut •

SYRIA

Tehran ■

JAMMU AND KASHMIR

Shikoku

LEBANON

Damascus ■

Kabul ■

Islamabad ■

Kyushu

ISRAEL

Baghdad ■

Amman ■

IRAQ

IRAN

R. Indus

HIMALAYAS

TIBETAN PLATEAU

Salween R.

Mekong R.

Yangtze River

Shanghai •

3

Jerusalem ■

JORDAN

New Delhi ■

Mount Everest

Chongqing •

Kuwait City ■

KUWAIT

PAKISTAN

NEPAL

Ryukyu Islands

BAHRAIN

Kathmandu ■

BHUTAN

Thimphu ■

Taipei ■

Tropic of Cancer

Riyadh ■

QATAR

R. Ganges

Dhaka ■

Hong Kong

TAIWAN

SAUDI ARABIA

UNITED ARAB EMIRATES

Muscat ■

INDIA

BANGLA-DESH

Kolkata ■

MYANMAR

Hanoi ■

Red Sea

OMAN

Irrawaddy R.

San'a ■

YEMEN REPUBLIC

• Mumbai

Arabian Sea

WESTERN GHATS

Bay of Bengal

Vientiane ■

LAOS

VIETNAM

South China Sea

Mount Nabi Shu'ayb

Yangon ■

THAILAND

Manila ■

Socotra

Bangkok ■

CAMBODIA

PHILIPPINES

Andaman Islands

Phnom Penh ■

2

Colombo •

SRI LANKA

Nicobar Islands

MALAYSIA

Mount Kinabalu

SEYCHELLES

MALDIVES

BRUNEI

Bandar Seri Begawan ■

Kuala Lumpur ■

SINGAPORE

Borneo

Sulawesi

Jaya Peak ▲

Sumatra

Jakarta ■

Java Sea

INDONESIA

Java

Dili ■

1

Equator

EAST TIMOR

Indian Ocean

B   **C**   **D**   **E**

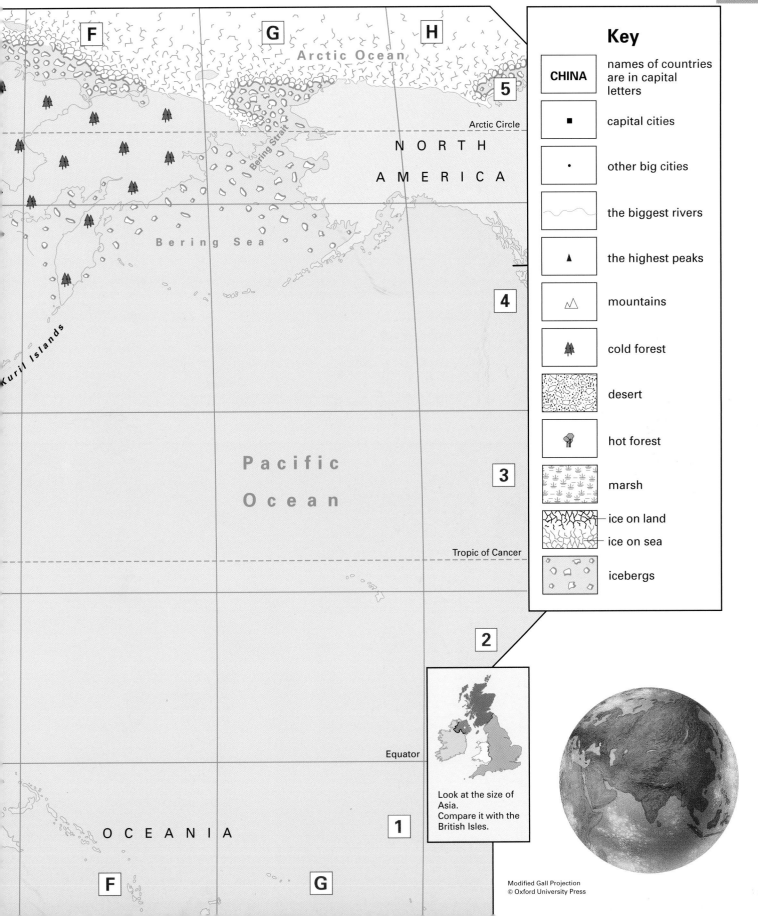

F

G

H

Arctic Ocean

5

Arctic Circle

N O R T H

A M E R I C A

Bering Strait

Bering Sea

4

Kuril Islands

Pacific

Ocean

3

Tropic of Cancer

2

Equator

Look at the size of
Asia.
Compare it with the
British Isles.

1

O C E A N I A

F

G

Key

CHINA	names of countries are in capital letters
■	capital cities
·	other big cities
	the biggest rivers
▲	the highest peaks
⋀	mountains
♠	cold forest
	desert
	hot forest
	marsh
	ice on land / ice on sea
	icebergs

Modified Gall Projection
© Oxford University Press

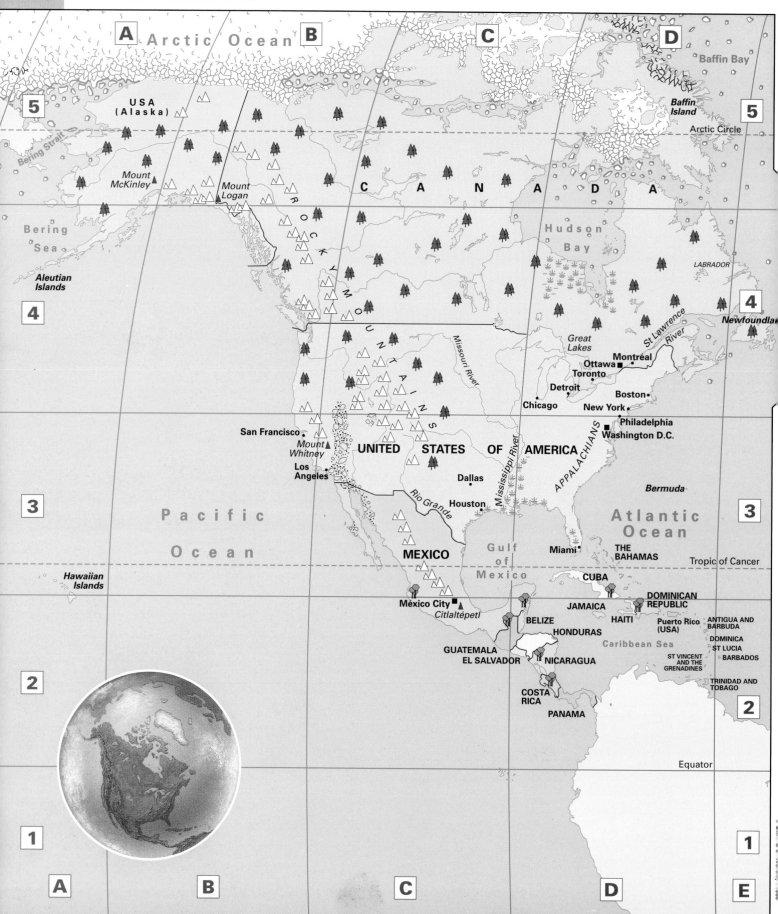

A   Arctic Ocean   B   C   D

Baffin Bay

5

USA
(Alaska)

Baffin
Island

Arctic Circle   **5**

Bering Strait

Mount
McKinley

Mount
Logan

C   A   N   A   D   A

Bering
Sea

Hudson
Bay

LABRADOR

Aleutian
Islands

4

R
O
C
K
Y

Great
Lakes

St Lawrence River

Newfoundla

4

M
O
U
N
T
A
I
N
S

Missouri River

Ottawa   Montreal

Toronto

Detroit

Chicago   Boston

New York

Philadelphia

San Francisco

Mount
Whitney

UNITED   STATES   OF   AMERICA

Washington D.C.

Los
Angeles

Dallas

Mississippi River

APPALACHIANS

Bermuda

3

Pacific

Ocean

Rio Grande

Houston

MEXICO

Gulf
of
Mexico

Miami

THE
BAHAMAS

Atlantic
Ocean

3

Tropic of Cancer

Hawaiian
Islands

CUBA

México City

Citlaltépetl

JAMAICA

DOMINICAN
REPUBLIC

HAITI   Puerto Rico
(USA)

ANTIGUA AND
BARBUDA

BELIZE

HONDURAS

Caribbean Sea

DOMINICA

ST LUCIA

2

GUATEMALA
EL SALVADOR

NICARAGUA

ST VINCENT
AND THE
GRENADINES

BARBADOS

TRINIDAD AND
TOBAGO

2

COSTA
RICA

PANAMA

Equator

1

1

A   B   C   D   E

Key

CUBA — names of countries are in capital letters

■ — capital cities

• — other big cities

— the biggest rivers

▲ — the highest peaks

⩜ — mountains

🌲 — cold forest

— desert

— savannah

🌳 — hot forest

— marsh

— ice on land
ice on sea

— icebergs

Look at the size of North America and the size of South America. Compare them with the British Isles.

A B C D

6 — Tropic of Cancer — 6

Atlantic Ocean

5

Caracas
VENEZUELA
River Orinoco
Georgetown
Paramaribo
GUYANA Cayenne
Bogotá SURINAME
COLOMBIA FRENCH GUIANA

Quito Equator
Galapagos Islands
ECUADOR Cotopaxi
Chimborazo
River Amazon

BRAZIL

ANDES

PERU

Lima

Lake Titicaca
La Paz Brasília
BOLIVIA
PARAGUAY Rio de Janeiro
Paraguay River River Paraná Tropic of Capricorn
São Paulo
Asunción

Pacific Ocean

ATACAMA DESERT

ANDES

URUGUAY
Mount Aconcagua
Juan Fernandez Islands
Santiago Buenos Aires Montevideo
CHILE ARGENTINA

Atlantic Ocean

Stanley
Falkland Islands

Southern Ocean Cape Horn

A B C D

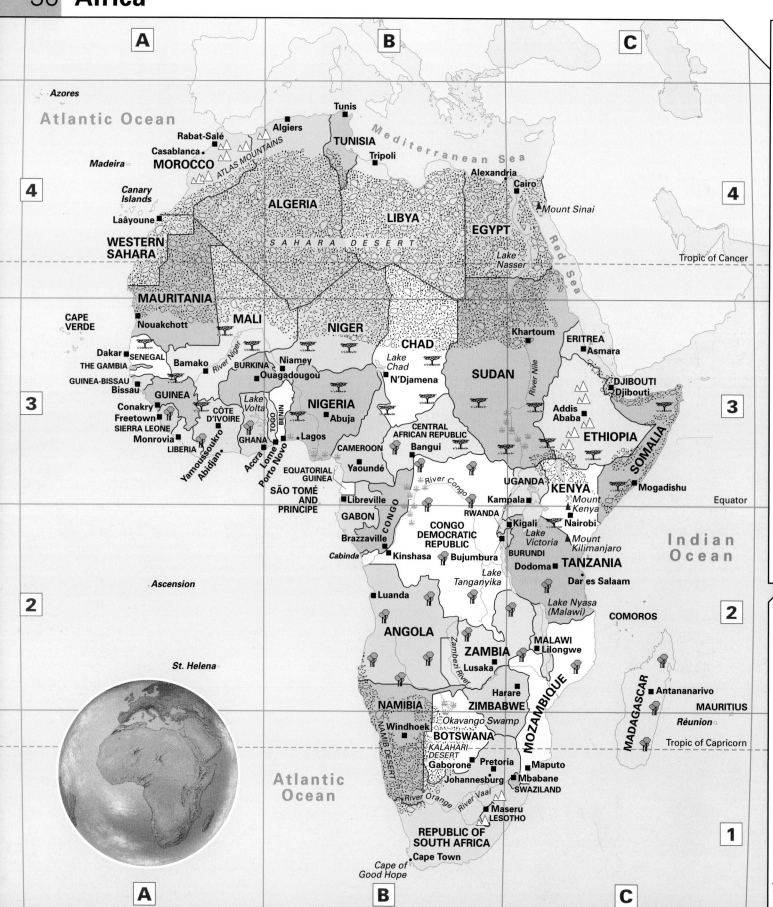

Azores

Atlantic Ocean

Tunis

Algiers
Rabat-Salé
Casablanca
MOROCCO
ATLAS MOUNTAINS
TUNISIA
Tripoli
Mediterranean Sea
Alexandria
Cairo

Madeira

Canary
Islands

Laâyoune
ALGERIA
LIBYA
EGYPT
Mount Sinai

**WESTERN
SAHARA**
SAHARA DESERT
*Lake
Nasser*
Red Sea

Tropic of Cancer

MAURITANIA
MALI
NIGER
CHAD
Khartoum
ERITREA
Asmara

CAPE
VERDE
Nouakchott
*Lake
Chad*
River Nile

Dakar
SENEGAL
Bamako
River Niger
BURKINA
Niamey
Ouagadougou
N'Djamena
SUDAN
Addis
Ababa
DJIBOUTI
Djibouti

THE GAMBIA
GUINEA-BISSAU
Bissau
GUINEA
*Lake
Volta*
NIGERIA
Abuja
ETHIOPIA
SOMALIA

Conakry
Freetown
SIERRA LEONE
Monrovia
LIBERIA
CÔTE
D'IVOIRE
GHANA
TOGO
BENIN
Lagos
CENTRAL
AFRICAN REPUBLIC
Bangui

Yamoussoukro
Abidjan
Accra
Lomé
Porto Novo
CAMEROON
Yaoundé
River Congo
UGANDA
KENYA
Mogadishu

Equator

EQUATORIAL
GUINEA
SÃO TOMÉ
AND
PRINCIPE
Libreville
CONGO
Kampala
*Mount
Kenya*

Ascension
GABON
Brazzaville
RWANDA
Kigali
Nairobi
*Mount
Kilimanjaro*

Cabinda
Kinshasa
**CONGO
DEMOCRATIC
REPUBLIC**
Bujumbura
*Lake
Victoria*
BURUNDI
TANZANIA
Dodoma
Dar es Salaam
**Indian
Ocean**

Luanda
*Lake
Tanganyika*

St. Helena
*Lake Nyasa
(Malawi)*
COMOROS

ANGOLA
MALAWI
Lilongwe

Zambezi River
ZAMBIA
Lusaka
MADAGASCAR
Antananarivo
MAURITIUS

Harare
MOZAMBIQUE
Réunion

NAMIBIA
ZIMBABWE
Okavango Swamp

Windhoek
NAMIB DESERT
BOTSWANA
Maputo
Tropic of Capricorn

*KALAHARI
DESERT*
Gaborone
Pretoria
Mbabane
SWAZILAND

**Atlantic
Ocean**
Johannesburg
River Orange
River Vaal
Maseru
LESOTHO

**REPUBLIC OF
SOUTH AFRICA**
Cape Town

*Cape of
Good Hope*

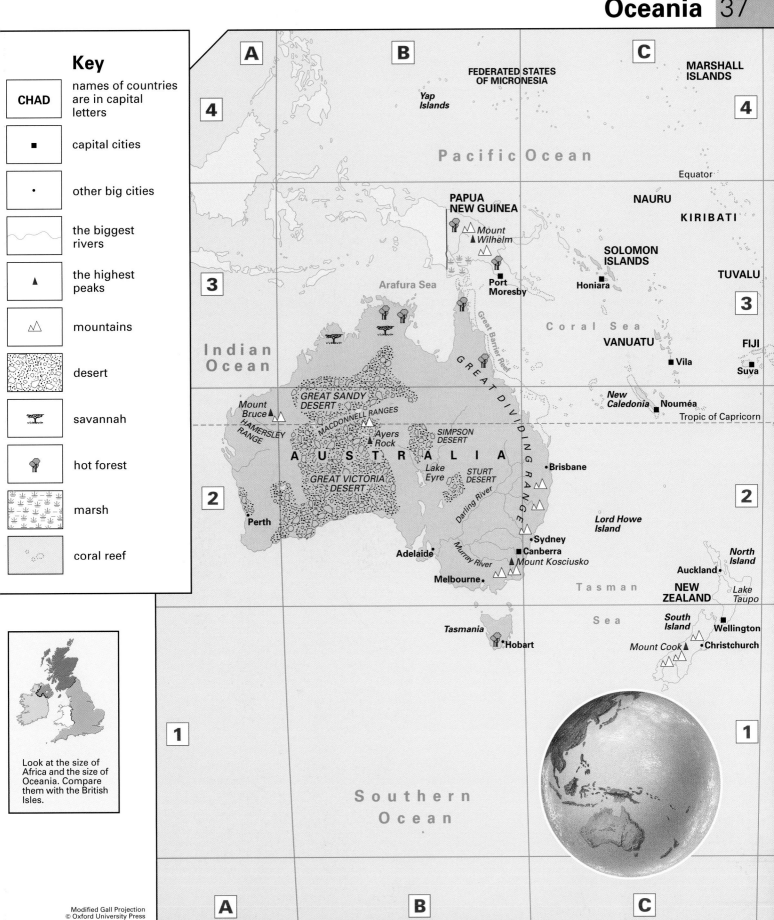

Key

CHAD	names of countries are in capital letters
■	capital cities
•	other big cities
	the biggest rivers
▲	the highest peaks
⩓	mountains
	desert
	savannah
	hot forest
	marsh
	coral reef

Look at the size of Africa and the size of Oceania. Compare them with the British Isles.

FEDERATED STATES OF MICRONESIA

Yap Islands

MARSHALL ISLANDS

Pacific Ocean

Equator

PAPUA NEW GUINEA

Mount Wilhelm ▲

NAURU

KIRIBATI

SOLOMON ISLANDS

Port Moresby ■

Honiara ■

TUVALU

Arafura Sea

Great Barrier Reef

Coral Sea

VANUATU

FIJI

Vila ■

Suva ■

Indian Ocean

New Caledonia

Nouméa ■

Tropic of Capricorn

Mount Bruce ▲

HAMERSLEY RANGE

GREAT SANDY DESERT

MACDONNELL RANGES

Ayers Rock ▲

SIMPSON DESERT

AUSTRALIA

GREAT VICTORIA DESERT

Lake Eyre

STURT DESERT

• Brisbane

GREAT DIVIDING RANGE

Lord Howe Island

Perth •

Darling River

Murray River

Adelaide •

• Sydney

■ Canberra

▲ Mount Kosciusko

Auckland •

North Island

Melbourne •

Tasman

NEW ZEALAND

Lake Taupo

Sea

South Island

Wellington ■

Tasmania

Mount Cook ▲

• Christchurch

• Hobart

Southern Ocean

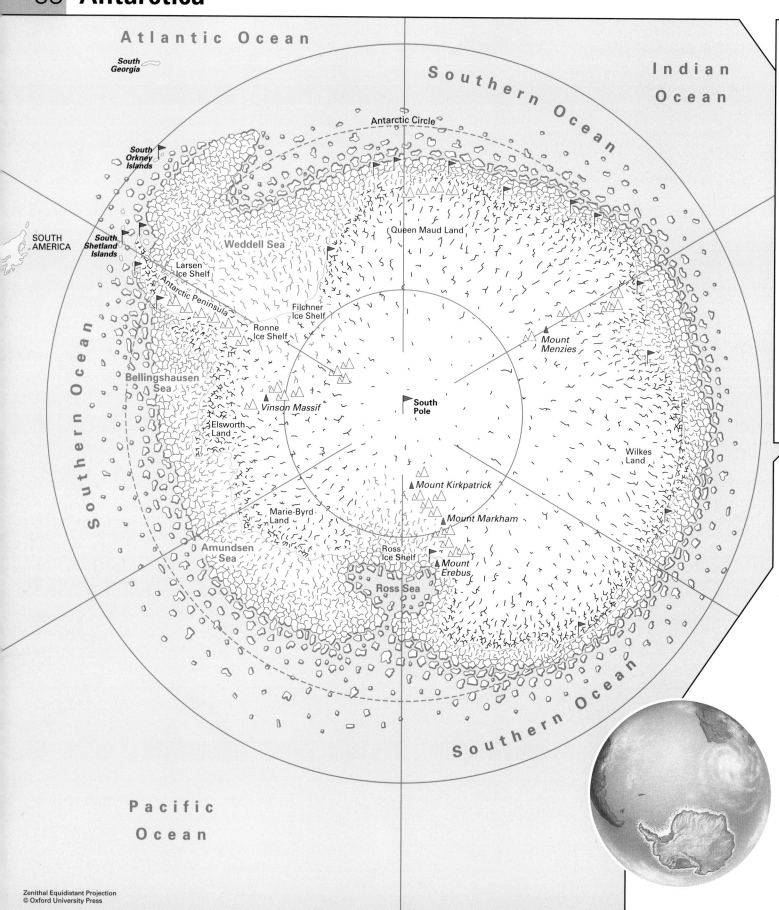

Atlantic Ocean

Southern Ocean

Indian Ocean

South Georgia

Antarctic Circle

South Orkney Islands

South America

South Shetland Islands

Queen Maud Land

Weddell Sea

Larsen Ice Shelf

Antarctic Peninsula

Filchner Ice Shelf

Ronne Ice Shelf

Mount Menzies

Bellingshausen Sea

Vinson Massif

South Pole

Elsworth Land

Wilkes Land

Mount Kirkpatrick

Marie-Byrd Land

Mount Markham

Amundsen Sea

Ross Ice Shelf

Mount Erebus

Ross Sea

Southern Ocean

Pacific Ocean

Southern Ocean

Zenithal Equidistant Projection
© Oxford University Press

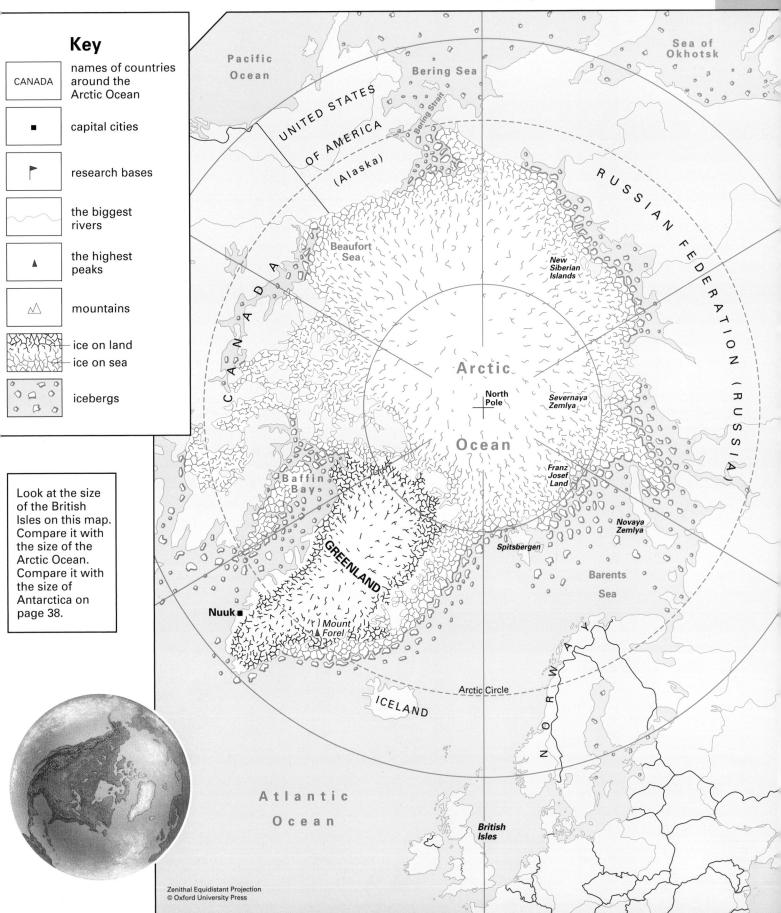

Key

CANADA — names of countries around the Arctic Ocean

■ — capital cities

⚑ — research bases

〰 — the biggest rivers

▲ — the highest peaks

⩕ — mountains

— ice on land
— ice on sea

— icebergs

Look at the size of the British Isles on this map. Compare it with the size of the Arctic Ocean. Compare it with the size of Antarctica on page 38.

Pacific Ocean

Sea of Okhotsk

Bering Sea

UNITED STATES OF AMERICA

(Alaska)

Bering Strait

RUSSIAN FEDERATION (RUSSIA)

CANADA

Beaufort Sea

New Siberian Islands

Arctic

North Pole

Severnaya Zemlya

Ocean

Baffin Bay

Franz Josef Land

Novaya Zemlya

Spitsbergen

GREENLAND

Barents Sea

Nuuk ■

▲ Mount Forel

NORWAY

Arctic Circle

ICELAND

Atlantic Ocean

British Isles

Zenithal Equidistant Projection
© Oxford University Press

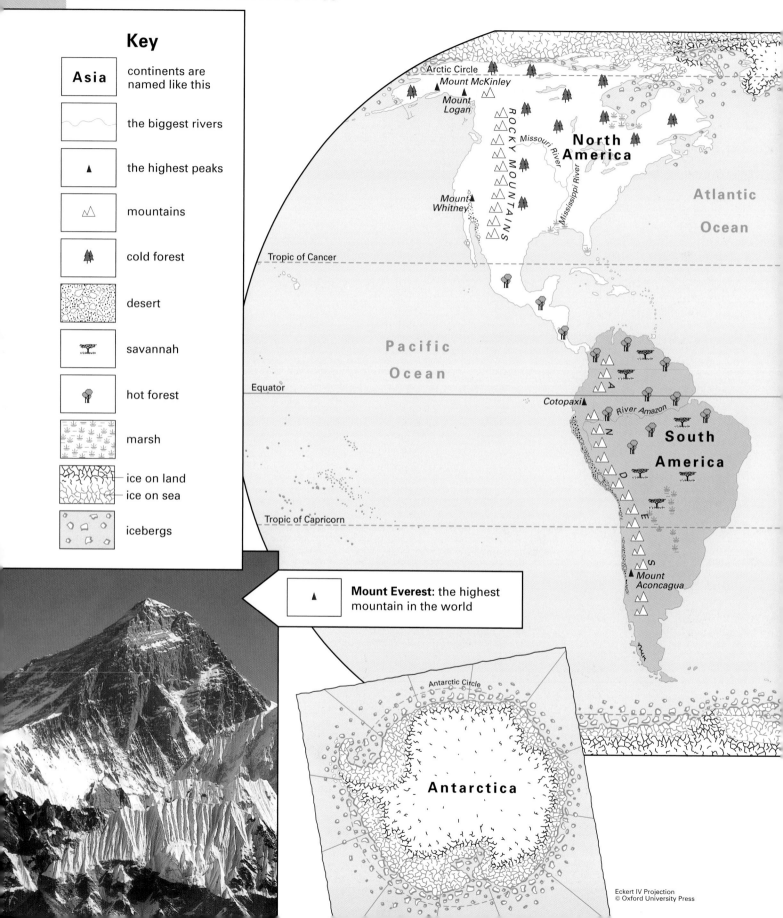

Key

Asia   continents are named like this

the biggest rivers

▲   the highest peaks

⌂   mountains

🌲   cold forest

desert

savannah

hot forest

marsh

ice on land
ice on sea

icebergs

▲ **Mount Everest:** the highest mountain in the world

Arctic Circle
Mount McKinley
Mount Logan ▲
ROCKY MOUNTAINS
Missouri River
North America
Mississippi River
Atlantic Ocean
Mount Whitney ▲
Tropic of Cancer
Equator
Pacific Ocean
Cotopaxi ▲
River Amazon
A
N
D
E
S
South America
Tropic of Capricorn
▲ *Mount Aconcagua*

Antarctic Circle
Antarctica

Eckert IV Projection
© Oxford University Press

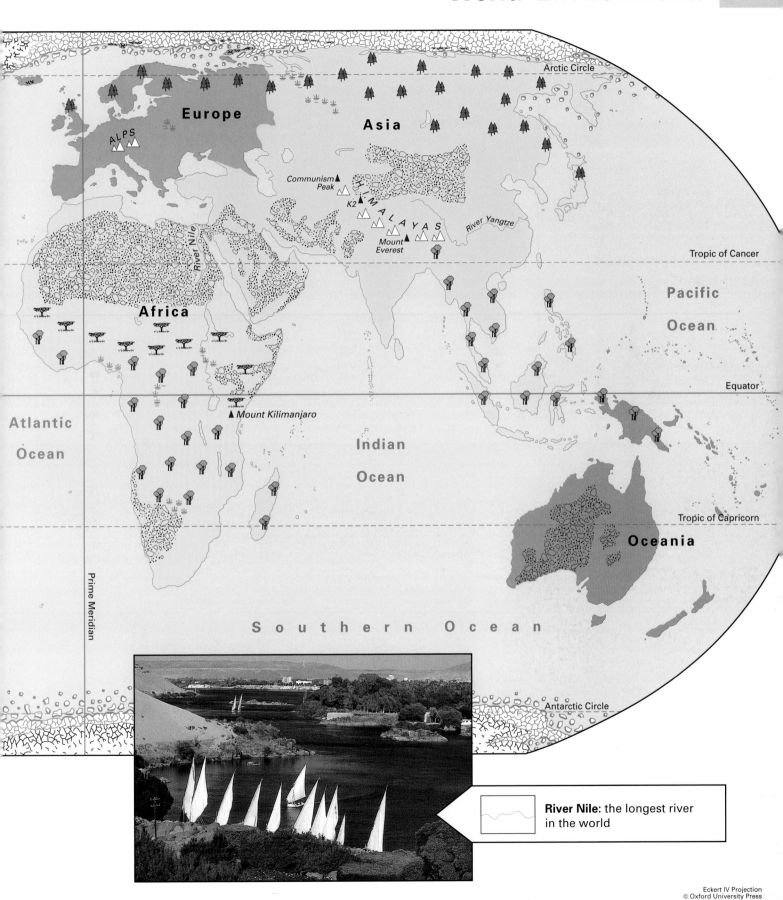

Arctic Circle

Europe

Asia

ALPS

Communism
Peak

K2

River Yangtze

Mount
Everest

Tropic of Cancer

River Nile

Africa

Pacific

Ocean

Mount Kilimanjaro

Equator

Atlantic

Ocean

Indian

Ocean

Tropic of Capricorn

Oceania

Prime Meridian

S o u t h e r n   O c e a n

Antarctic Circle

River Nile: the longest river
in the world

Eckert IV Projection
© Oxford University Press

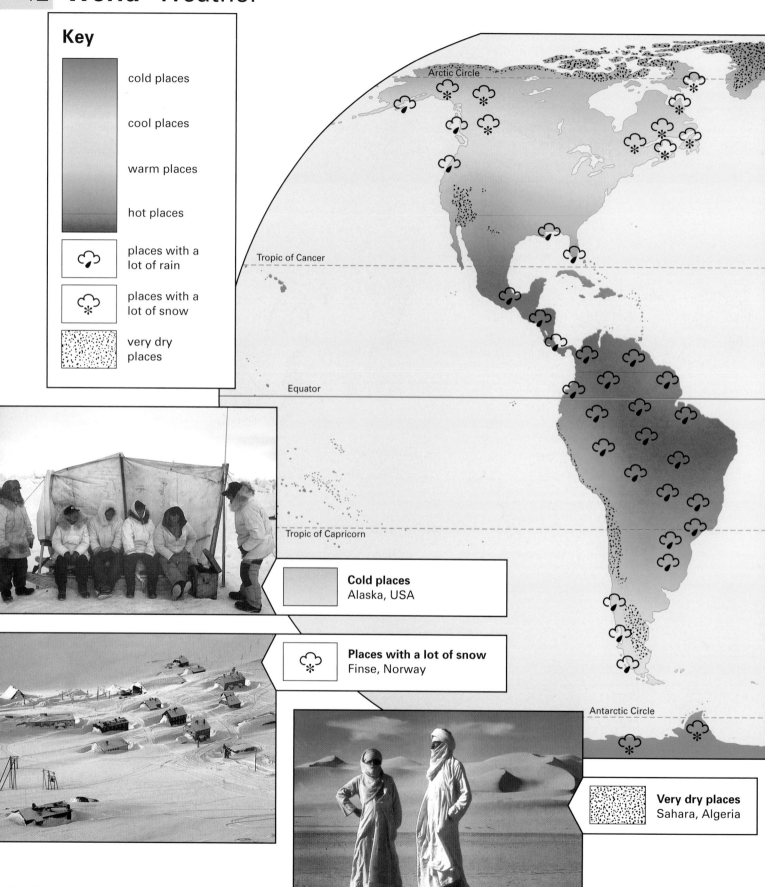

Key

cold places

cool places

warm places

hot places

places with a lot of rain

places with a lot of snow

very dry places

Cold places
Alaska, USA

Places with a lot of snow
Finse, Norway

Very dry places
Sahara, Algeria

Arctic Circle

Tropic of Cancer

Equator

Tropic of Capricorn

Antarctic Circle

Eckert IV Projection
© Oxford University Press

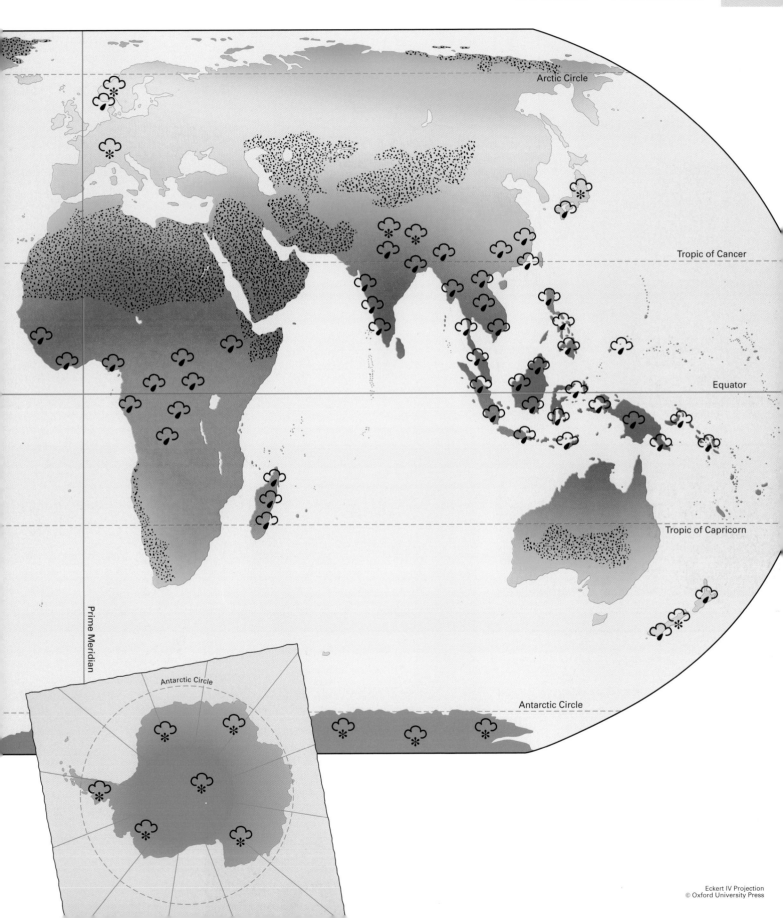

Key

one million (1 000 000) people live near each dot

○ the world's largest cities

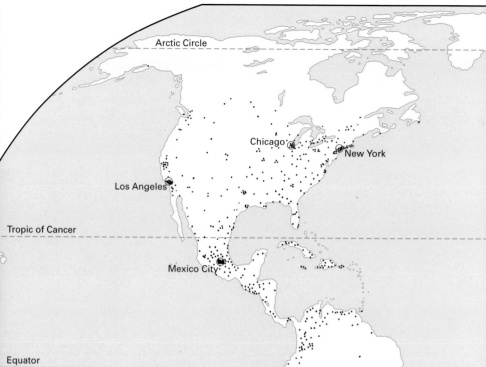

Arctic Circle

Chicago
New York
Los Angeles
Tropic of Cancer
Mexico City
Equator
Tropic of Capricorn
São Paulo
Buenos Aires
Antarctic Circle

Places where very many people live.
Tokyo, Japan

Places where very few people live.
Shetland Islands, Scotland

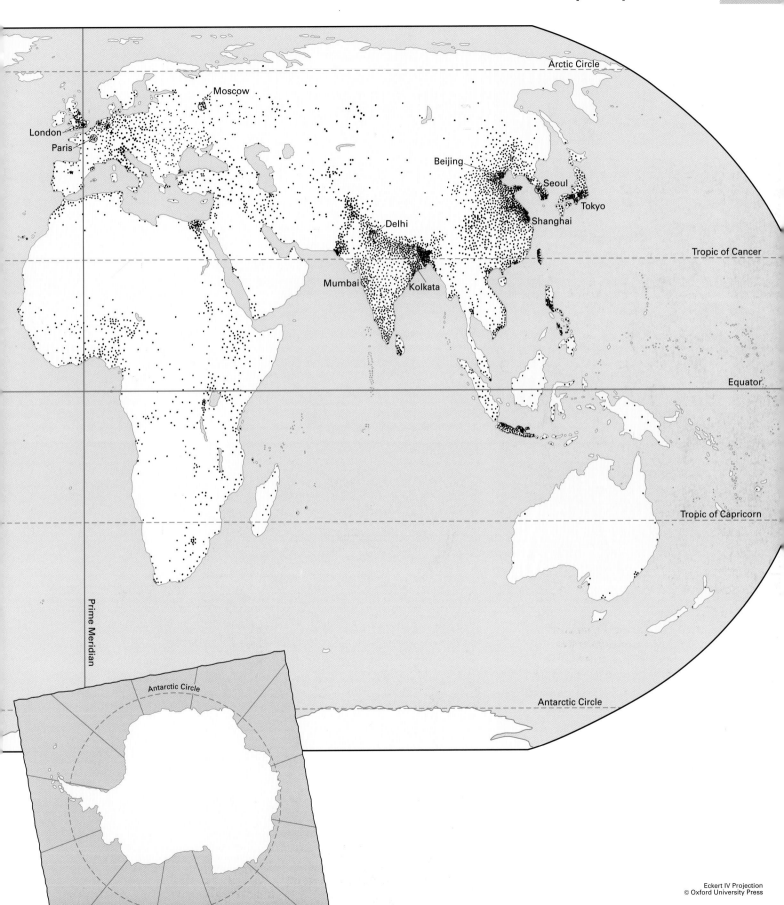

London
Paris
Moscow
Beijing
Seoul
Tokyo
Shanghai
Delhi
Mumbai
Kolkata

Arctic Circle
Tropic of Cancer
Equator
Tropic of Capricorn
Antarctic Circle

Prime Meridian

Antarctic Circle

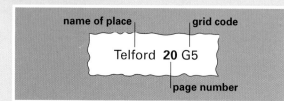